30-DAY PRESCRIPTION FOR SELF LOVE:

A Practical guide to self-love for those busy adults who are looking for real results.

May you find peace, happiness, success, and abundance in all that you do. May the sun always be peaked in the sky for you. May the stars in your life shine brightly. May you find kindness and acceptance in everyone you meet. May you find the love you deserve.

Written and concept by
Cordelia Prapaga with Gondora Official

FOREWORD

My massive gratitude to you, for not only purchasing this 30-day self-love and empowerment program, but also for beginning this journey of self-awareness, self-empowerment, and self-love. We are in an amazing day and time, The Age of Aquarius. The Aquarian shift has us all wanting to better ourselves, to find our wholeness, and become the best version of "ME" that we can be. Depending on where you are in your development, you could be working on any number of things: Finances, Mental Health, finding balance. We know now that there are many ways to get there: through meditation, positive thought, and Energy work. But what we need to understand as humankind is that there is only so far we can go in our development of ourselves until we learn to love ourselves.

Self-love can be a bit of a taboo subject for some people. We are coming from a Pisces Paradigm that says that self-love is egotistical and wrong. As we are learning, this type of mind frame or thinking couldn't be more wrong.

Is there a way to love yourself without allowing Ego and Arrogance to take over? The answer to that is yes! We absolutely can love ourselves, maintain our dignity and our self-pride, without allowing Ego to take over. This 30-day program will surely help you in your journey of self-discovery and self-love.

With all the love and energy that I can muster in my heart, I send you well wishes on your journey.

DEDICATION

Dedicated to my children. May I teach you in a way that you know your self-worth when you grow up. May you be happy and loved, always. May you know how much I treasure, love, and adore every single thing about you. May you know how truly precious you are in my eyes. May you know that everything I did in life, I did it for you. May you know that you are my sun, moon, and stars. You are the life's blood that runs through my veins.

TABLE OF CONTENTS

How to work the program

HOW TO WORK THE PROGRAM

Make sure you take the time, every day, to read your current lesson and take action. There is no time limit on each lesson. You might finish a lesson in one day, or a week. Go at your pace. There are questions and spaces for writing after each lesson. It is there for you to be honest and upfront with yourself about what you need to work on, change, or think about.

The entire point of this program is to DO. This is a program calling for you to take action in your life and ultimately make it better.

At the end of the Lessons are some adult coloring pages you can color to release stress and some SELF-LOVE worksheets.

DON'T
MAKE
YOURSELF
SMALLER
TO MAKE
SOMEONE
FEEL
BETTER

LESSON 1: AFFIRMATIONS

*C*ongratulations, friend. Today is the first day of the rest of your life. Take a moment to breathe in the new air, calm yourself, and thank the universe or the god/goddess of your understanding for taking you on this path.

I'll wait.

After you have taken a moment for a few deep breathes and to be grateful, let's begin, shall we?

Affirmations have a harmonious effect on your conscious and subconscious mind. Affirmations can truly be powerful if you use them correctly. Today we are going to go over a few self-love affirmations you can say to yourself every day. Then there will be a small activity and some space in the end to write some affirmations you feel passionate about.

Affirmations For Self-Love:

I am in love with my body.

I always make the right choices for myself.

I always choose to do activities that make me happy.

I am true to myself.

I am whole.

I always express gratitude for my working body.

I always express gratitude for my healthy body.

I love everything about me.

The people around me love me for who I truly am.

I speak my truth.

I am an empowered being.

I am empowered to take steps today to make a better future for myself.

The secret to making affirmations work harder for you is this:

When you say the affirmations, make sure you imagine opening all your chakras and pores, and imagine all those affirmations as vibrations. Then imagine those vibrations penetrating into your charkra points and pores, deep into your skin and your DNA. Make these affirmations a part of who you are.

YOUR ACTIVITY FOR TODAY:

1. Get some paper and tape, or post-it notes. Write down the following and place it somewhere you will see it when you first awake in the morning.

We are in this together. I chose you. I work for you. I love you. Let's work together for the benefit of us.

2. Also on some paper or post-it notes, write down a few affirmations you feel you need right now. Stick them up in various places around the house where they are visible. In your journey throughout the day, as you run across these post-it notes, take a deep breath to calm your mind and read the affirmations.

Affirmations I enjoy:

Take a moment to write down a few affirmations that will help you in this journey.

"ABOVE ALL,
BE TRUE TO
YOURSELF,
AND IF YOU
CANNOT
PUT YOUR
HEART IN
IT, TAKE
YOURSELF
OUT OF IT."

LESSON 2: ME TIME

*I*n this day and age where we have so many commitments, it can get easy to fall into a mundane pattern of constant stress. Commitments to work, kids, school, meal planning, grocery shopping, ETC. It is an absolute MUST to take time out for yourself every single day. I cannot stress this enough. It is such a small and seemingly insignificant task, but it will give you the daily boost you need.

Commit yourself to 10 minutes of "Me" time, three times a day. If you can go outside, barefoot, in the sun for that 10 minutes, even better. Commit to it. Don't make excuses. By doing this, you are showing the universe that you are truly ready for change.

YOUR ACTIVITY FOR THE DAY:

Make sure you take out 10 minutes, 3 times a day, for you and what you want. Do you want to use that 10 minutes to groom yourself? Sit outside in the sun? Meditate? (Gender specific) Paint your nails?

Commit to you. Take the time out for yourself.

Me time ideas:

Know Your Worth

LESSON 3: BODY LOVE

The true you is Spirit. Your body is your vehicle. Most people treat their vehicle better than they do their body, and if this is true for you, then this habit changes today. I want you to remember something; there is no such thing as perfection. The way the media portrays women and even men in specific body shapes, or features of the face, perfect skin, ETC, does not mean that you have to be what they portray. Fall in love with your body today because it sure does take the brunt of everyday life. Hate your upper arms? There are people who don't have arms and would love to have your arms. Hate your stomach? Your stomach is what processes all your food. It is part of what gives you height. Don't like your skin tone? It doesn't matter what skin tone you have. There is someone out there who is unhappy with theirs and are altering themselves to look like you. Realize that YOU are your own perfection.

YOUR ACTIVITY FOR TODAY:

Praise your body all day today. Praise how beautiful your unique eyes are. Praise the gap between your teeth. Praise your little toes. Praise your body for being healthy. Most importantly, give your body the gratitude it deserves! Your body does a lot. It processes food into energy, your feet hold up all your weight so you can walk, your back keeps your body aligned. Be grateful for all your body does for you. Take a moment to express that gratitude, and let your body feel your gratitude.

What I love about my body:

_____

_____

_____

_____

_____

_____

_____

_____

_____

_____

( ) SMART
( ) PRETTY
( ) INDEPENDENT
(x) ALL OF THEM

LESSON 4: LIVING IN THE "NOW"/ MIND LOVE

*I*t's important to have the right frame of mind. Ultimately, your frame of mind is what creates your thoughts, and your thoughts create your reality. So, we want to keep a healthy, positive mind and environment for our mind to thrive. How do you do it? You live in the Now. When you live in the past or the future, you experience anxiety, stress, and sometimes depression. When you live in the now, and recognize all you are blessed with *now*, you will feel much better.

YOUR ACTIVITY FOR TODAY:

Live in the Now. This can be hard for people to do; however, how you become a master is by practicing. Practice being in the now all day today. Don't get upset at yourself if you forget. Remember, this is a new journey for you. Place a rubber band around your arm (not too tight) with the intention that every time you see it, you put yourself in the now. Smell your surroundings. Look at what's in front of you.

What are you doing right now? How is it making you feel? Express gratitude for it. If you find yourself restless or upset at any time, see Lesson 6, because there is clearly a "trigger" that needs to be addressed and cleared.

List of things I can do to put me in the "Now":

Make it your
goal to fall in
love

with everything that
you are

LESSON 5: DRESS FOR SUCCESS

There are a number of individuals who believe that "Dressing for Success" means you have to have a $400.00 name brand outfit with shoes and accessories to match. This couldn't be more untrue. I feel just as good in my second-hand outfit from the thrift store as I do my business attire. Dressing for success is more of a mind frame than it is an excuse to buy super expensive clothing.

What To Look For When Putting Together Or Buying An Outfit:

-Make sure you wear clothing that matches your personality.

-Wear stuff that, when you put it on, you feel fantastic and ready to start your day.

-Wear clothing that makes you feel energetic and youthful.

-After you put it on, look in the mirror. If you love your outfit, you're good to go!

. . .

The reason wearing clothing that makes you feel good is so important, is because your clothing is an extension of you. An extension of your mind frame. An extension of your success. Think about it. Do you ever see anyone who is successful and happy wearing articles of clothing that are dirty and wrinkled? No. It's not about how much you spend on your clothes that matters. It's how you treat them and how you feel in them.

Make sure you also treat your clothing well. Wash them, fold them, and when needed, iron them. Keeping good care of your clothing will extend better energy and more self-confidence around you. It also emotionally feels better when you are wearing clothing that is clean and taken care of. Wearing clothes that make you feel good also works with the Law of Attraction, in the sense that if you feel good, you're attracting good things to you.

There is no reason why you shouldn't dress for success. Even if you are a stay at home mom, or dad, wear something casual and trendy. Something that makes you feel good while you're at home running around with the kiddos.

YOUR ACTIVITY FOR TODAY:

-Go through your clothing and give away anything that doesn't make you feel happy when you hold it or wear it. Donate anything that doesn't make the cut.

-Fold all your clothing and make sure they are in clean, neat, folded piles or hung up.

-If you are able to, buy a few new pieces that make you feel happy and youthful. If you don't have the money right now, start putting away a few dollars every week so you can make a small purchase soon. It doesn't have to be anything big or expensive, and there are always clearance sales online or in stores.

Any thoughts or comments on today's Lesson? Write them here:

BE YOURSELF TODAY,

YOU LOOK BEAUTIFUL LIKE THAT

LESSON 6: ADDRESSING THE ISSUES

We all have issues going on within us that we need to work on. But due to the nature of society, we don't know how to work through our issues without turning to medication, or even self-medicating with toxic substances. How do we work on our issues? Well, first, you need to know what your issues are. Maybe you are already somewhat self-aware and know you have, let's say for example, issues with anger. This is a start. But to truly target the core issue, you must know what is causing your anger. What is the core issue causing you to be angry? Here is how you work through it, find the core issues, and release them.

You can use this activity with any upsetting feeling you may experience, but for now, we will continue using the "Anger" scenario. For this lesson, and for future lessons and any new triggers, you'll need to have a notebook specifically for writing your trigger releases so you can look back through the pages at the end of the 30 days, or year, and see how far you've come.

. . .

Example:

You're doing dishes and something happens that triggers your anger. Maybe you drop an expensive serving plate that was given to you by someone you deeply care for. This triggers an angry reaction. Take a moment to sit down and feel that anger. Take out your notebook and write down every feeling you feel. Go deeper than just anger. Ask yourself all the emotions and feelings you are feeling. For example: Let's say the deeper issue triggering your anger is that you are worried you won't have enough money to replace it. Then, maybe along with anger, you feel guilty, unworthy, or depressed. Really reach inside of that anger and pull out every emotion you are feeling. Once you have written them all down, make an affirmation for each feeling and start saying those affirmations throughout the day. Here is what that list might look like:

Anger - I am allowing myself to work through my anger instead of allowing it to control me.

Guilty - I am abundant and able to easily replace anything I need to.

Unworthy - I am worthy of all the good things that life has to offer.

Depressed - I am proactively doing things daily to make me a happier person.

Once you've finished listing the emotions and affirmations, take a quiet moment to breathe a few deep breaths. Once you feel calmer, imagine opening your pores and chakra points, clearing them of all those old negative emotions, and filling that new space with the affirmations.

Do this every single time you are triggered with a negative emotion, and you will find yourself working through your issues and becoming happier. It is important you do this because you are showing yourself that you are indeed worth the work.

YOUR ACTIVITY FOR THE DAY:

Whenever you feel yourself getting triggered throughout the day, make sure you take the necessary time to pinpoint the core emotions. Once you've realized the emotions, create affirmations to assist you with the healing process, and then do the quick meditation mentioned above.

I would also like to mention that this should be done every day, not just today.

Any thoughts or comments on today's Lesson? Write them here:

(If you don't have a notebook yet, that you can dedicate to your emotional releases and affirmations, use this page until you can get one.)

To be beautiful means to be yourself.
You don't need to be accepted by others.
You need to accept yourself

LESSON 7: WHAT MAKES ME FEEL GOOD?

*I*t is important that you are doing things every single day that make you feel good. For me, these things are having a clean environment, cooking, smelling good, and lighting scented candles. So, I make sure to incorporate all these things into my daily activities. When I go out, I purchase perfumes and candles that I love to smell around the house or on myself. These are small things that make me happy and ultimately make my day better. Take time today to really list all the things that make you happy. These aren't things you have to do every day, but maybe some of the things you list are activities you can do weekly. For example, I absolutely love bubble baths, but I only have time for a bubble bath once a month. If I am lucky, I'll be able to take one once a week. With that said, list the things that make you feel happy and incorporate them into your daily/weekly/monthly schedule.

YOUR ACTIVITY FOR THE DAY:

List everything that makes you happy and make sure to do 2-3 of those activities today.

List of activities that make me feel good:

----

darling just believe in yourself

LESSON 8: GETTING RID OF WHAT NO LONGER SERVES ME: PEOPLE

Getting rid of all that no longer serves you can be not only a big task but an emotional one. So, this will be a recurring theme over the next few lessons. Today is the "people" edition.

It is important to have people around us who lift us up, who make us feel good, who love and support us and want to see us win. If there is anyone in your life who doesn't represent those qualities in your life, it is time to let them go. You have gone through enough negative experiences in your life; it is time to live happily. Part of living happily means having positive people around you. If you are around people who are constantly dragging you down, they are not your friend and they are also not beneficial to your growth.

YOUR ACTIVITY FOR TODAY:

To anyone who doesn't believe in you, puts you down, or makes you feel bad:

Delete their number. Delete their texts or messages. Block them if you need to. Block them from emailing you, texting you, calling you. You are worthy of having quality and loving friends around you. Start today.

Take a moment to write down what qualities and attributes you would like your future friends to have:

Dear Self;

I know you're doing
the best you can.
I believe in you.
Keep going.

Love Me xo

LESSON 9: GETTING RID OF WHAT NO LONGER SERVES ME: SOCIAL MEDIA

Continuing with the "What no longer serves me" theme, let's take it even further. Unless you have been living under a rock, you know what social media is, and more than likely you are part of it. We have Twitter, Facebook, Instagram, and so many other platforms that are being used now days.

Just like it is important to have people around us that lift us up and make us feel good when we are around them, it is important to have a social media that reflects what we want to experience in our lives. If there are any pages you currently follow or like that trigger you, either delete those pages from your "likes" or mute them. You can mute them by going to the page and "unfollowing" the page without unliking it. If there are any groups you are in that trigger you, do the same. As for people, do the same thing. You don't have to delete them off your page if you don't feel comfortable; you can always unfollow them.

YOUR ACTIVITY FOR TODAY:

Go through all your social media accounts and delete, unlike, or unfollow anything that no longer serves you, or that triggers you or makes you feel bad.

Take a moment to reflect on what you learned today and what you would like to achieve by cleaning up your social media:

Dip yourself into a pool of self-love, and you'll never drown from other people's judgements about you.

LESSON 10: GETTING RID OF WHAT NO LONGER SERVES ME: MATERIAL ITEMS

*D*ay 3 of the "What no longer serves me" theme, and we are on a roll. First and foremost, good job on getting this far. Getting rid of people and situations that no longer serve you can be quite emotional for some people. It's a shedding of energy, and there can be a bit of mourning that goes along with the necessary change. But remember that even though you may be emotional about it now, things will and do get better. It's a necessary step you have to do in order to evolve.

Today, we are getting rid of material items that no longer serve you. Make sure that you give yourself enough time to do this. If you have a lot of stuff, this process may take a few days, or even a few weeks. But it is important to do this lesson thoroughly before you go into Lesson 11, because Lesson 11 is a continuation of lesson 10.

Having a bunch of stuff lying around the house, stuffed into closets, or even over-filled boxes lining your basement walls is stuck energy that needs to be released. It is important not to have all this "stuck" energy around your personal space, clogging up new energy that is trying to come in. All this stuff you have lying around could also be a representation of what is energetically going on in your head. If your head space is full, your surroundings will be full. Let's try to take the next few hours, days, or weeks to clear this space up.

YOUR ACTIVITY FOR TODAY:

Go through your entire house: closets, drawers, cupboards, under the bed, etc. Get rid of anything that:

1. Has no meaning to you

2. Hasn't been worn or used in the last year

Then go through your car, truck, or SUV and do the same thing.

Donate all of it to charity, have a yard sale, or sell it on eBay.

Take a moment to reflect on the items you have given away or sold and write a little about how it has made you feel to get rid of all the extra material items you no longer need.

AND ONE DAY SHE
DISCOVERED THAT
SHE WAS FIERCE,
AND STRONG,
AND FULL OF FIRE,
AND THAT NOT EVEN
SHE COULD HOLD
HERSELF BACK
BECAUSE HER
PASSION BURNED
BRIGHTER THAN
HER FEARS.

LESSON 11: ORGANIZING MY SPACE

So far in this quest, you are making changes to your mainframe and your surroundings to show self-love. Now that you have done all that Material and Social Media clearing, you are ready to organize your surroundings. You may be wondering how organizing your space shows self-love. It's quite simple really. What are you saying to yourself if you live in a dirty and unorganized space? You're saying that you are unworthy of a clean space to live and thrive in. No one who truly loves themselves lives in untidy surroundings.

YOUR ACTIVITY FOR TODAY:

Go through your house and organize everything. If you want some new and interesting ideas of how to organize certain areas of your house, YouTube and Pinterest can serve as great resources for helpful ideas. I can't tell you how many times I have watched organizing videos on YouTube, and I learn new ways to organize every single time. Tidy up your drawers, closets, cupboards, and everything else. Then organize your purse, your makeup space, and your car.

What new thing did you learn about yourself today while you organized your space?

_____

_____

_____

_____

_____

_____

_____

_____

_____

_____

_____

_____

Eat like
you
love yourself.

LESSON 12: MOVING MY BEAUTIFUL BODY

I have read several articles recently about how exercise affects your mind frame and how the future of a healthy mindset is exercise. You can read multiple articles about exercise and how it affects your mental health, and it is all true. Moving your body is important, not only for your physical health but for your mental health as well.

There are many of us who hear the word "exercise" and automatically droop down and sigh. Exercise, for some people, is not a fun word due to either the pain they experience when they move or just because "exercise" isn't something they like to do. But with that said, exercise doesn't have to be boring. Exercise doesn't have to be a treadmill and weights. Exercising your body and moving your body should only be done in ways that you find fun. Maybe you like the treadmill and the weights, or maybe you are more of an interpretive dance type of a person. Do things that you love doing. Also, wear an outfit that makes you feel good while you move your body.

. . .

Example:

When I started working out, it was on the elliptical, and I found that I could not bear to be on the elliptical for longer than 6-7 minutes. This was not due to endurance issues, but I just couldn't do it. There was some sort of block stopping me from going any further. Being on the elliptical for 6-7 minutes felt like an eternity. So, I started asking myself what I enjoy doing. I love dancing, I love walking outside, and I love hiking in nature. Therefore, these are the things I started doing to get my exercise in. For doing the dishes or cooking, I put together a playlist that I could listen to in the background. With the music going, while I was cleaning, I could just dance and dance and dance. The next thing I knew, I was working up a sweat. Moving my body helped me loosen up my joints and feel better overall. I would also have specific outfits that I wore just for working out so that I felt good about myself and how I looked when moving my body.

YOUR ACTIVITY FOR TODAY:

1. Pick out a few outfits that you would like to wear while you move your body.
2. Put together a playlist of fun songs you enjoy. (You can make a free playlist on YouTube, use Spotify, a CD, or whatever music apps you like to use.)
3. If you are trying to lose weight, get a few inspirational photos from magazines or print them from your computer.
4. List some body moving ideas you would like to try.

List some activities you would like to try when it comes to moving your body. What sounds fun? It can be

anything from dancing to weights, or even going to a playground.

Encourage yourself, believe in yourself, and love yourself. Never doubt who YOU are.

LESSON 13: HOW TO CHANGE THE THINGS I DISLIKE

When it comes to self-love, it is important not to force things upon yourself that you dislike doing. This lesson can be tricky to navigate if some of the things you dislike are things like your job, or your living situation. However, keep in mind that not all the things you dislike can be fixed in a day or even a week, but it is important to be clear about the things you dislike and make a definitive plan to fix them.

YOUR ACTIVITY FOR TODAY:

1. I want you to be perfectly clear on what you dislike.
2. Make a plan on how to change the things you dislike.

Things I dislike and my plan of action to change those things:

Dislike: _____

Plan of action in changing it:

_____

_____

_____

Dislike: _____

Plan of action in changing it:

_____

_____

_____

Dislike: _____

Plan of action in changing it:

_____

_____

Dislike: _____

Plan of action in changing it:

Dislike: _____

Plan of action in changing it:

Dislike: _____

Plan of action in changing it:

Dislike: _____

Plan of action in changing it:

Examine what you tolerate.

LESSON 14: DEEP BREATH/LEARN HOW TO RELAX

*L*oving yourself also means learning how to relax. With the world being as fast paced as it is, we are always rushing to the store, rushing to make dinner, rushing the kids here or there. WE are always in a rush; SOCIETY is in a rush. Just stop. Now. Take a few very deep breaths. Learn how to take time every day to relax. It's important we make time to be in a calm environment. It is important for our mental health, our body's health, our nervous system, and even our relationships, to relax. Love yourself today and every day by learning how to relax. Relaxing can be as simple as a morning routine with candles, music, and yoga. It could be a nighttime routine of soft music while you wash your face. It could be a midday routine of treating yourself to some Vitamin D in the sun for a few minutes.

YOUR ACTIVITY FOR TODAY:

Write down some fun, relaxing activities you can do to experience daily relaxation and stick to it. Do something relaxing every single day.

Activities I can do daily to experience relaxation and how I can integrate these activities into my daily life:

"FOCUS ON YOU."

LESSON 15: BEING SELF-EMPOWERED: KNOWING MY LIMITS

*B*e empowered is understanding that you have limits, and that is okay. There are a lot of us who overwork ourselves or over exhaust ourselves (emotionally, financially, and physically) to help other people. There is absolutely nothing wrong with helping other people; in fact, helping other people is an act of service we should all be doing. However, with that said, don't over exert yourself in ways that will end up hurting you in the end. Over exerting yourself isn't good for you or anyone else in your life. It makes you stressed, cranky, depressed, etc. Be very clear as to what your limits are and don't go over that.

Even if it is something as simple as emotional exhaustion. If you're having a day where things seem to be going left, and everything you are involved with isn't going the way you want it to, that has an emotional and mental effect on you. You can tend to get frustrated as the day goes on. Recognize your limits. Take a break, release whatever negative energy is inside of you, and fill yourself with positive energy. During the day, your "positive energy" cup may run dry. Fill it back up.

YOUR ACTIVITY FOR TODAY:

As you go through your day, recognize your limits and honor them.

List some limits you have and how you will change the way you interact with some people who have surpassed your limits:

LIFE IS SO
BEAUTIFUL

LESSON 16: BEING SELF-EMPOWERED: ALWAYS SPEAKING MY TRUTH

*L*ying or being dishonest doesn't do anyone any good. in fact, it does more harm in the end. Part of being a self-empowered individual is always speaking your truth, even if someone may not like it. If the relationship (friendship or romantic) you have with someone can break simply by you speaking your truth, then the foundation of that relationship would have never lasted long to begin with. It should also be said that just because you should speak your truth, doesn't mean you have to be rude about it. Always speak your truth, but speak it in such a way that you are kind about it.

YOUR ACTIVITY FOR TODAY:

Be aware of every word coming out of your mouth. Am I being honest? Am I being kind? If I find myself being dishonest with someone, why is that? Maybe this person isn't a safe person to be around and speak my truth with, and if that is the case, I should seriously consider what type of energy they bring into my life and whether or not I want that for the future.

Any notes about this lesson can be written here:

'To love oneself
is the beginning
of a life-long
romance.'

LESSON 17: BEING SELF-EMPOWERED: TAKING CONTROL OVER MY LIFE

*W*e have all been in a situation where we have given others control over our lives when we didn't want to, and it didn't feel good, did it? I remember when I was living in Nevada and I became friends with my next-door neighbor. I remember her being a nice person, but she was really pushy. Me, being the pushover that I was at the time, allowed her to make my decisions for me even though it made me uncomfortable. It got to the point where I despised our friendship and no longer wanted to hang out with her. One thing I remember the most was when she didn't approve of my driving and asked for my keys so she could drive. I told her no, that I would drive and it would be fine. She got visibly annoyed and said, "No, no, we're not driving like grandmas today. Let me drive." Her getting annoyed like that scared me, and I ended up giving her the keys. It made me sick to think about the fact that she would be driving my only family vehicle. In fact, still today, as I recollect that story, I can feel how I felt in that car as she drove, my stomach in knots and worried about losing my only means of transportation. My fear of her disapproval was more than my fear of losing my family vehicle. Once I recognized that about myself, it took a lot of healing and work, but I got myself to a point where I no longer allowed people to put me in a situation like that. I became self-empowered and took control over my life.

YOUR ACTIVITY FOR TODAY:

Become self-aware today. Say a self-empowerment affirmation every day, and even throughout the day, that will assist you with your self-empowerment. If there is any specific downfall you have, such as peer pressure or agreeing to things you don't want to do because you're afraid about other's perception of you, find an affirmation to help you with it. Post those affirmations around the house and say them every day, multiple times a day.

My favorite self-empowerment affirmations:

Give a few examples....

I am stronger than other people's opinions.

I can make my own decisions.

I don't need the approval of others.

NEVER LOVE
ANYONE WHO
TREATS YOU LIKE
YOU'RE ORDINARY.

LESSON 18: BEING SELF-EMPOWERED: WHAT DO I WANT IN MY FUTURE?

This is a very straight forward question. What do you want in your future? What do you want your future to look like? Be very detailed here. What kind of home do you see yourself in? What type of romantic relationship? What kind of friends will you have in your life? What about your job, your income? Be empowered to make the necessary steps today, to bring yourself the future you want.

YOUR ACTIVITY FOR TODAY:

Make a list of what you want in your future and a list of steps you can do today, tomorrow, and even next week and month, in order to get you where you want to be.

What I want in my future:

Steps I can take now:

What I want in my future:

Steps I can take now:

What I want in my future:

Steps I can take now:

What I want in my future:

Steps I can take now:

What I want in my future:

Steps I can take now:

Note to Self:

Begin loving yourself.

Its never too late.

LESSON 19: SELF-AWARENESS: TOOTING MY OWN HORN

*K*nowing what you are good at is a wonderful thing. You should never feel bad about tooting your own horn. Many of us, growing up, were told that we shouldn't engage in this type of behavior due to the fact it makes you look self-centered or conceited. I feel this is partly why so many people have issues accepting compliments or have self-esteem issues. Let's change this aspect.

Your body is physical and energy vibrations. Yes, it's made of flesh and bone, and your body also does a lot for you. Your arms hold your children, and your legs walk you from place to place. Your eyes behold the glory of the sun and the stars. Be grateful for all these beautiful things you are able to do with your body and mind. As mentioned above, your body is also a vibrational energy source, and when it is complimented and given the love and attention it deserves, your body tends to react to that love by healing, working better, and feeling better.

YOUR ACTIVITY FOR TODAY:

1. Recognize what you're good at and comment on it. You can either say it out loud, talk about it on Facebook, or say it in your head. Do it in a way where you are honoring yourself, and not in a way that you are trying to put anyone else down. It's all about intention. If your intention is good, then all is well, but if you are doing it to make someone else feel bad, this is the wrong way of doing it.

Example:

You have an uncanny ability to be able to find major deals, sales, and discounts. You never pay full price for anything. You're always running into huge sales and getting the best items on sale. Pat yourself on the back. You did a fantastic job. Good for you. Congratulate yourself and feel your physical body react to that support and love you are giving it.

2. Accept all the compliments you get about yourself, today and every day. If someone compliments you, instead of refusing that compliment, say, "Thank you," or even, "Thank you, I love that about myself also." Your body reacts to these things, and your body will feel good because you are accepting compliments about it instead of refusing them.

Write down some amazing things you are good at. Compliment yourself:

----

iT'S NOT YOUR
JOB TO LiKE ME.
iT'S MiNE.

LESSON 20: SELF-AWARENESS: SELF-APPRECIATION

*M*y goal today is to have you KNOWING what you're grateful for, and also FEELING that gratitude. I always tell people that there IS a difference between knowing and feeling, and in order to be truly grateful, you must do both. Also, in order to manifest, you must be able to do both. Knowing things you're grateful for is the equivalent of having a boat. It'll get you to your destination eventually... But Feeling what you're grateful for is the equivalent of having a boat with a jet pack attached to it. You are going to get to that destination much faster.

YOUR ACTIVITY FOR TODAY:

I want you to really feel the gratitude you have for YOU. What do you do every day for your family, your siblings, for people/customers/coworkers at work? What do you do every day at home? Be grateful for the working hands that assist you with cutting up your food, your beautiful feet that get you to and from places, your working body. Be grateful for your persistence, your kindness. Be grateful for your working mind. Write them all down, and then go into meditation and feel them.

What is it about YOU that you are grateful for?

"Don't try to
lessen
yourself for
the world;
let the
world catch
up to you"

LESSON 21: SELF-AWARENESS: VISION BOARD

*W*hat better way to show yourself you love yourself, than a little art and self-expression? Today, you are creating your vision board. Put everything on it that you want to experience, including what you want your body to look like, where you want to travel, how you want to feel, things you want to experience, etc. Keep this board in a place where you can see it every day.

YOUR ACTIVITY FOR TODAY:

Get a cardboard box, or a poster board and some magazines, or print some photos off from your computer, and create a vision board. Get creative. Use markers to write in affirmations or motivational quotes, draw hearts or polka dots, and decorate the entire board. Have fun.

Some ideas for my Vision Board:

Rise above it all. It's time to soar.

LESSON 22: TIME TO TREAT YOURSELF

Treating yourself isn't a bad thing. it's an awesome thing! We should treat ourselves from time to time, with whatever it is in the moment that will make us happy. Do you want a new purse, to go to the movies, or to have that ice cream shake you have been eyeballing for a while now? Today is the day to do it! Make sure that while you are treating yourself, you are fully aware of your worthiness to do so. Put out an intention that while you enjoy this treat, you are doing it out of self-love.

YOUR ACTIVITY FOR TODAY:

Treat yourself to anything you want with the intention that you deserve it.

How am I going to treat myself today?

FALL IN LOVE
WITH TAKING
CARE OF YOURSELF.
MIND-BODY. SPIRIT.

LESSON 23: ART/CREATIVE DAY

*S*how yourself love today by creating a space to let you explore Art in any way you see fit. There have been many articles written about how art and being creative assists with stress levels, mental health, and healing. Let's not forget that art is also fun.

YOUR ACTIVITY FOR TODAY:

Today is a day to allow your inner, creative self to shine in any way you choose. I enjoy my creative days with changes to my makeup, my hair, and my nails. I do my own nails so I get creative with designs, colors, and even rhinestones. I try out a hairstyle I have been wanting to try, or use different makeup colors. These activities I mentioned above are my creative outlets, but they don't have to be yours. Yours could be making your own healthy toothpaste, mouthwash, or even making your own scented and colored candles. It could be painting, drawing, or coloring. Use your time today to be creative.

. . .

What are some fun art projects I would like to do?

Dear Self,
I choose you,
and only you
I am sorrry it
took so long

LESSON 24: TAKE A DAY OFF AND PLAN AN ADVENTURE

When is the last time you had an adventure? Most of us in adulthood haven't had an adventure in a long time. Our days consist of taking care of our four-legged babies, or our two-legged babies, work, house, and responsibilities. How long can a person go on like this without getting bored with life and allowing this boring life to consume them until they are depressed? Don't allow that to happen.

YOUR ACTIVITY FOR TODAY:

Find time today, and at least once every month, or every week if you can, to have an adventure. Your adventures don't even have to cost you anything. Do you frequently go on hikes and jogs? Go somewhere new and exciting this time. Do you go to a specific gym every single day? Today, go to a gym that is 2 hours away, and enjoy the ride, listen to music. Google the best restaurant list in your state, so find one you haven't been to and go there. Never tried East Indian food, well today is the day to do it!

What are some adventures I would like to do over the next year?

Walk boldly
in the
direction of
your dreams.

LESSON 25: SHAKE THE BOOTY, JUDY!

*T*he lesson name! If you're giggling, good. :) Life is to be enjoyed. When I first wrote the Lesson, I just had to insert the "Judy" part because it gave me a good laugh. Show your body and your mind some love today by shaking your booty to some good music. And when I say shake your booty, I don't mean twerking. But hey, if that is your thing, then go for it. The only rule? Have fun! By doing this, you are showing life who is boss. You are having fun and enjoying your time. You're also activating the endorphins in your brain.

Endorphins=Happiness

What a better way to show yourself some love than experiencing happiness?

YOUR ACTIVITY FOR TODAY:

Dance around in any manner you want. Play the music loud, and go ahead and sing, too!

My favorite music and dance moves are:

You are loved.
You are wonderfully made.
You are beautiful.
You have purpose.
You are a masterpiece.
God has a great plan for you.

LESSON 26: TODAY, I STOP PROCRASTINATING

STOP PROCRASTINATING. Take steps every single day to make yourself a better you. To bring yourself where you want to be in life. To give yourself positive experiences. To heal your inner darkness and your inner demons. Why? Because YOU deserve it! When you procrastinate, you are prolonging your happiness and you are prolonging all the things you deserve.

YOUR ACTIVITY FOR TODAY:

Take a moment today to write down all the things you have been procrastinating and then DO THEM. Figure out the block that is stopping you from getting these things done and get rid of it so you can move on.

What am I procrastinating and what can I do to move forward?

You are worth
taking
time for.

Self care
is a necessity,
not a
luxury.

LESSON 27: LOTION DOWN AND BUBBLE BATH

*B*ubble Baths sound so wonderful, don't they? Unfortunately, we, as adults, don't have enough of them. Our kids get more bubble baths than we do. Kids really know how to have fun and live life carefree, don't they? Kids are truly the most beautiful people in the world with their big hearts and creative spirits. But enough about that, we are working on our self-love. Show your body you care and that you love and support it by giving it a bubble bath and a lotion down.

YOUR ACTIVITY FOR TODAY:

Take time out today, or this week, to have a good soak in some scented bubble bath or even bath salts. When you get out, use your favorite lotion to rub all over yourself. Don't have a bath tub? Take a long shower or do a foot spa. If you have the extra money, you can rent a hotel with bath tub in it. I have a tub, but it isn't a large soaking type tub, so once month, I rent a hotel room with a big tub and do a staycation. A staycation is when you go on vacation but you stay in your city or state. Some will go on staycations in their state but in a different city.

Never taken a staycation before? When you have some extra money, try it.

Where would I like to go on staycation, and what would I like to do?

'Your self-worth is determined by you. You don't have to depend on someone telling you who you are.'

LESSON 28: FORGIVE YOURSELF

*T*his is an important lesson. Forgive yourself. We all harbor what ifs and situations we were a part of that we have a hard time forgiving ourselves for. Well, it's time to forgive. No matter what it is, forgive yourself. It's time! Maybe you harbor self-hate for things you did when you were a child, or teen. Or, maybe, in your eyes, you weren't the best parent or weren't the best partner to your husband or wife. It's time to let that all go. We all make mistakes. No one is perfect. By holding on to those things, we are ultimately holding ourselves back. Really dive deep on this one. If you harbor self-hate because of something you are not in control of, such as a disease or sickness, don't keep it hidden out of shame. Just say it and release it.

YOUR ACTIVITY FOR TODAY:

Take time out to go into meditation today and visually point out all the self-hate you are experiencing. Visually point out the feelings, the regrets, the hurt, and then visually turn those things into light and allow them to float away. Then verbally forgive yourself.

How do I feel now that I have forgiven myself?

YOUR
RELATIONSHIP
WITH
YOURSELF
SETS THE
TONE FOR
EVERY OTHER
RELATIONSHIP
YOU HAVE.

LESSON 29: A DAY WITHOUT ANY COMPLAINTS

*A*s beings of light, complaining ultimately brings us down, both energetically and mentally. They say that if you stop complaining altogether and only speak about things you are grateful for or things you love, everything around you starts shifting. Let's start today. This is Day 1 of no complaining. Let's also add no yelling. Some people are yellers, and some aren't. That's okay. Yelling is a sign of frustration. Let's bring more positivity into our lives by decreasing the negativity. Show yourself love by living a more positive verbal lifestyle.

YOUR ACTIVITY FOR TODAY:

1. Today is Day 1 of no complaining and no yelling. Stay conscious about what you are feeling. If you start to feel frustrated, use your words to speak with the person you are frustrated with. If it is a child you are frustrated with, try kneeling to their level and talking to them in a very matter of fact tone, and make yourself clear. Even try taking away privileges until you are being listened to. Be empowered to change the narrative. You can do this. Once you do Day 1, continue on to Day 2 and so on and so forth.

2. Every time your phone rings today, express your gratitude for something, anything. Once you get in the habit of not complaining and also constantly expressing your gratitude, you will see so many shifts in your life.

3. For each day you go without complaints, check off the days below. You can also reward yourself by giving yourself a dollar a day (or whatever you can afford). Then, once you have enough money saved up for a staycation or a treat, go do it. :)

Day 1 __

Day 2 __

Day 3 __

Day 4 __

Day 5 __

Day 6 __

Day 7 __

Day 8 __

Day 9 __

Day 10 __

Day 11 __

Day 12 __

Day 13 __

Day 14 __

Day 15 __

Day 16 __

Day 17 __

Day 18 __

Day 19 __

Day 20 __

Day 21 __

Day 22 __

Time to
unlearn
everything
society has
taught you
about hating
your body.

LESSON 30: NO MORE APOLOGIZING

Since you are now speaking your truth in a kind way (LESSON 16), there is no longer any reason for you to apologize for anything. Let me go over this a little bit so there is no misunderstanding.

Once you are an empowered and kind human being that speaks your truth in a kind and loving manor, there will be nothing for you to apologize for. Stop apologizing for being late or being honest. If you're late, there was a reason. If people can't understand that, that is on them. Don't apologize for not having a "Martha Stewart" clean home. There are extenuating circumstances in which that is not possible. And, certainly, do not apologize for being yourself or for having a mind of your own!

If there were issues in the past, before you became the empowered and loving individual you are today, such as name calling or any derogatory behavior, these are the things you apologize for.

YOUR ACTIVITY FOR TODAY:

Pay attention to how you are feeling and what you are saying. Don't apologize for anything you meant or said (so long as it was honest and said in a kind way), and don't apologize for anything that is out of your control or not your fault.

Now that you have reached the end of the book, how do you feel?

----

111 SELF LOVE IDEAS

Use these idea's daily, and especially on days when you are struggling.

---

1. **Meditate or find a quiet place to relax.**
2. **Drink plenty of water. What better way to show your body you love it than to nourish it?**
3. **Stretch.** – Before you start your day, take a few minutes for a good muscle stretch.
4. **Stop procrastinating.** – Procrastination is a form of perfectionism. Accept that it's not going to be perfect.
5. **Listen to your inner voice.** – It's important to listen to your own head and heart.
6. **Cut yourself some slack.** – Possibly the most important tip on this list. We hold ourselves to impossible standards and then beat ourselves up when we don't meet them. Would you be this hard on anyone else?

7. **Slow down.** – Stop and take a breath. While out and about today, stop and smell the flowers.

8. **Identify your passion.** – What do you love? Do more of it.

9. **Schedule some "me time" in your calendar.**

10. **Call a friend and reminisce.**

11. **Declutter.** – You should have ONLY the stuff that you love. Purge everything in your life, both physical and emotional, that you don't honestly need, use, or love. (This also includes social media, work, and people.)

12. **Toot your own horn.** – You're awesome. Please make sure everyone knows it.

13. **Find a mantra or an affirmation that lifts your spirits.**

14. **Stand tall.** – You feel much more powerful when you stand up straight and don't slouch.

15. **Make a list of all the things you love about your body.** – It feels good to love yourself.

16. **Get a massage.**

17. **Move your body.** – The only limitation: it has to be fun. Don't get on a treadmill if you hate the treadmill.

18. **Invest in really good bras.** – This one is specifically for the ladies. You feel better when you look fantastic

19. **Purge things that aren't good for you.** – Unhealthy foods, cigarettes, a miserable work environment, toxic people, Facebook page, etc.

20. **Limit your news consumption.** – It's important to be well-informed, but the non-stop feed of earthquakes and plane crashes and economic crisis and war is not good for us. Be deliberate in finding the balance that's best for you. Once you've seen today's news cycle, turn it off.

21. **Say yes to life.** – Opportunities are everywhere. Take a class, join a team, go bungee jumping.

22. **Get creative.** – Draw, paint, sew.
23. **Put a post-it on your mirror that says, "You look beautiful!"**
24. **Buy fresh flowers for yourself every now and then.**
25. **Use colored pens for no particular reason.** – Blue and black are fine, but how about orange, blue, and pink?
26. **Take a walk without a destination.**
27. **Take a hot bath with bubbles or bath salts.**
28. **Write in a journal.**
29. **List the things that you're grateful for.** – You can't help but feel better when you literally count your blessings.
30. **List the things that you like about yourself.**
31. **Color in an adult coloring book, the ones with intricate designs and lots of detail.**
32. **Spend time with people who make you happy.**
33. **Take an entire day to enjoy your kids.**
34. **Rub your favorite lotion all over yourself while you express gratitude for your healthy body.**
35. **Buy a new perfume or body spray.**
36. **Stay up late one night and enjoy star/moon gazing.**
37. **Create something.** – Try making your own toothpaste, or deodorant.
38. **Treat yourself to something you've been wanting.**
39. **Smile at yourself in the mirror every morning and name one thing you love about yourself.**
40. **Squash negative thoughts.**
41. **Try something new.** – Do that thing you've always wanted to try. The more experiences you have, the richer your life will be.

42. **Get enough sleep.** – Everything is hard when you're tired.

43. **Say no.** – Your time is valuable. Set boundaries.

44. **Ask for a hug.** – We all need one. :)

45. **Hire out/ask for help.** – Hire someone to mow the lawn or scrub the floors. Teach the kids to do laundry. Give that project to a co-worker. You do not have to do it all.

46. **Take a deep breath.** – And another. Now another. It's like a mini-break to reset yourself during the day.

47. **Light a candle or use a reed diffuser.** – Your sense of smell creates the strongest memories. Find scents you love and enjoy them.

48. **Claim some space for yourself.** – A place where you can go to have a quiet moment to read a book, or meditate, or cry – somewhere that you can get some peace and privacy.

49. **Get out into nature.** – Reconnecting with the earth is just good for your soul. Feel the breeze. Breathe the fresh air. So good!

50. **Buy the good ice cream.**

51. **Use lotions & soaps with scents that you love.** – It's a nice way to pamper yourself.

52. **Give a compliment.** – Telling someone that they had a fantastic idea or that they look beautiful in that color creates a pleasant environment and makes two people feel good for the price of one.

53. **Listen to music.** – Listen to whatever makes you happy.

54. **Take pride in yourself.**

55. **Let someone else be in charge for a while.** – Other people can be responsible while you do something for yourself.

56. **Don't answer the phone unless it's someone you want to talk to right now.** – Some people find it

difficult not to answer a ringing phone, but it's liberating once you learn to ignore it or, even better, just turn it off.

57. **Have faith.** – It's going to work out. The future is bright!

58. **Take time to write a bucket list.**

59. **Go on a retreat.** – For a couple of minutes or a couple of days, get away for a bit to re-energize.

60. **Set out some time for a quality hair mask.**

61. **Use moisturizer on your skin.**

62. **Find a good way to blow off steam.** – Don't bottle it up.

63. **Take time to find out who you are as a person.**

64. **Spend some time alone for quiet reflection.** Try stopping to think about your life, your goals, and your dreams.

65. **Keep your words positive.** – Happiness and complaints cannot coexist.

66. **Let light and fresh air into your house.**

67. **Turn off your e-mail, cell phone, blackberry, fax, etc. for a while.**

68. **Pare down your to-do list.** – Feeling overwhelmed? What's on your list that can wait or that you can ask someone else to do?

69. **Avoid boredom.** – Keep your brain active to keep the blues at bay. Puzzles, games, etc.

70. **Make your home a haven.** – Your home should be a place where you can take a breath and really relax.

71. **Be stingy with your time and energy.**

72. **Play.** – A board game, a sport, finger painting.

73. **Eat foods that you love.**

74. **Be silly every now and again.**

75. **Laugh.**

76. **Limit screen time.** – Too much time in front of computers, TVs, video games, and blackberries (or all of the

above) disconnects you from the world immediately around you and makes your brain mushy. Make sure that you're getting plenty of input from the non-virtual world.

77. **Be present.** – Be deliberate about experiencing what's happening right now. It's all about the journey – don't miss yours!

78. **Laugh.** – Go to a comedy club or watch stand-up comedy on Netflix.

79. **Trust yourself.** – You are smart, capable, and talented. Your choices are just as valid as anyone else's. Don't second guess yourself.

80. **Do something that's only for you.** Have a hobby? Do it.

81. **Make sure your health is in order.** Get the vitamins and supplements you need or want to try.

82. **Redecorate an area of your home that you didn't love before.**

83. **Wear something fancy.**

84. **Stay off social media for a day.**

85. **Organize your area.**

86. **Stand up for yourself.**

87. **Celebrate! (for any reason at all)** – Your kid learned to tie his shoes! Let's party!

88. **Choose optimism.** – Thinking positive thoughts has an impact on your day and on your life.

89. **Take time out to visualize what you want in life**

90. **Tune out the Negative Nancies.**

91. **Add color to your surroundings with items like flowers or paintings.**

92. **Surround yourself with the things you love.** – Frame photos of loved ones that bring happy memories. You should have the stuff that you love all around you.

93. **Stop hating your body. Find new ways to love your body.**

94. **Sing loudly.** – In the shower and the car and anywhere else you like. With reckless abandon.

95. **Get a foot massage or a pedicure.**

96. **Tell someone you love them.** It matters.

97. **Take all of your vacation and sick days.** – You earned them.

98. **Play hooky.** – Call in sick once in a while when you're not sick. Use the day to pamper yourself (not to catch up on errands or housework).

99. **Let go of anything that weighs you down, including material items.**

100. **Minimize multi-tasking.** Multi-tasking can cause a lot of stress. The house doesn't have to be "Martha Stewart" clean all the time.

101. **Break your routine once in a while.**

102. **Get out!** – Get a gym membership or take a ballet class, or even take a walk in nature.

103. **Make your bed an oasis!** – Put those satin sheets on your bed, and the microfiber blankets. Use whatever feels the best against your skin and make your bed a heavenly place to sleep.

104. **Say a Gratitude Prayer.** – It feels good to verbalize all the things you're grateful for.

105. **Go on a drive.** – Whether it is long or short, take yourself on a drive while listening to some music and enjoy your surroundings.

106. **Pamper yourself with a new purchase or self-care task.** – Want to get your nails done? Need a new hair cut? Go for it!

107. **Take a night off and watch your favorite 80s or 90s movie.**

108. **Eat your favorite food.** – Take one meal and make it the best.

109. **Place affirmation post-it's around the house.** – Take your favorite 10-15 affirmations on self-love and place them in areas you will see them. Every time you see one, say it out loud and accept it.

110. **Do something fun today.** – Whether it's exercise, a long bath, dyeing your hair, or spending time with your dog, enjoy the moment.

111. **Instead of cooking dinner, hire out or eat out.** – You can find healthy options out there, including various salads and low carb options. Whatever your diet is, you can stay on it while still treating yourself to a meal you didn't have to cook.

LIST OF AFFIRMATIONS FOR
SELF-LOVE

On rough days, use EFT tapping to really allow the meditations to sink in. EFT tapping doesn't have to be as complicated as you see on Youtube, and you don't have to buy and read a 300 page book to correctly do EFT tapping. Keep it easy and simple. It's all about the intent behind the tapping, not so much the tapping it self.

Begin by taking a few deep breaths.

Close your eyes.

Open and clear your Chakra's:

Imagine your Chakra's opening, and white light coming from the heavens to open them up and heal them.

Say your Affirmations while tapping on your third eye, your temples, or your chest bone in between your breasts.

Affirmations:

. . .

For anxiety:

I love everything about myself

I am allowing myself to heal

I am always finding new ways to love myself

I am finding gratitude in the moment

I am always paying attention to the now

Everything I am worried about is already taken care of

I am enough

Body Love:

I am enough

I am beautiful

I am strong

I am living an easy life

I am naturally carefree because my life is easy

I am finding new things to love about myself

When I look at myself in the mirror, I love who I see

I love every curve

Self worth Affirmations:

I approve of myself. I love myself deeply and fully

I am forgiving of myself and others

I am worthy of love and joy

I am worthy of healthy living

My life is a gift

I take responsibility for who I am: The bad and the good.

Affirmations for attracting positive relationships into your life:

I am always experiencing positive interactions with others

I will surround myself with positive people

The people I am around, bring out the best in me

The people around me are loving and kind

Affirmations for self-esteem

I am healthy

I am well groomed and confident

My inner peace and harmony is matched my my outer well-being

I do not need anyone else to feel happy and fulfilled, I express those feelings for myself naturally

My imperfections make me unique and special

I am enough, just as I am

You can see a full list of Affirmations on www.gondoraofficial.com/affirmations

RECOURSES FOR SELF-LOVE

Self Love Habits:

Mirror Time- Look into the mirror, deep into your eyes and say the following sentences that you resinate with the most.

(*Insert your name here*) IS *beautiful*

(*Insert your name here*) IS *a warrior*

(*Insert your name here*) IS *kind-hearted*

(*Insert your name here*) IS *loving*

(*Insert your name here*) IS *strong*

(*Insert your name here*) IS *faithful*

(*Insert your name here*) IS *creating his/her future*

(*Insert your name here*) IS *being kind to myself*

(*Insert your name here*) IS *having kind thoughts about myself*

(*Insert your name here*) IS *patient with myself*

(*Insert your name here*) IS *focused*

(*Insert your name here*) IS *perfect just as I am*

(*Insert your name here*) IS *always inspired*

(*Insert your name here*) IS *constantly expressing gratitude*

Lotion Time:

Find a lotion with a scent that you really love. Lotion your body up while saying why you love that specific part.

I love my stomach because it held my children while pregnant (or - it digests the good food I eat)

I love my legs because they hold the weight of my body while I walk. They get me to and from where I need to go.

I love my arms because with them I am able to hug the ones I love.

I love my feet because they give me balance.

I love my hands because they allow me to touch.

I love my beautiful beating heart because it is what keeps me alive.

I love my face because it makes me unique.

I love my skin because it is strong and beautiful.

I love my eye's because with them I can see beautiful colors.

I love my neck and my voice because with it, I am able to speak my truth.

Reframing negative memories:

Take back control over the negative memories that have drained so much energy out of you by doing this simple exercise.

When ever a negative memory surfaces go to a safe, and quiet area where you can lay down or sit with your back strait. Take deep breaths. Imagine a bright light over your head coming down through your crown chakra and throughout your entire body. Imagine that light bringing up the memory and all the emotions behind that memory. Now name the negative emotions you feel. Once you have named these negative emotions, allow the light to take that negative emotion back up through your crown chakra and into the light to break up. Tell yourself that you are now free of any negative emotion or belief system behind that memory.

. . .

Self-Awareness

I am good at:

I am at my best when:

What do I love about myself?:

What I need to work on:

What I am most proud of:

What I love the most about my personality:

What I love the most about my body:

I am working on and healing:

What I regret the most and how I can come to terms with it:

How I can show myself love everyday:

. . .

Who do I trust and why?:

My fondest memory:

Who Am I?

What do I want my future to look like?

What are my goals in life?

Am I living true to myself? If not, what can I do to start living my truth?

What am I holding onto that I need to let go?

What are my passions in life?

What would be my ideal career choice?

Do I care about what others think about me? What can I do to change that?

Who was my first love?

.   .   .

Who do I love now?

List the things that make me feel good:

Who was my first crush?:

What words do I need to hear right now?:

What's my favorite high school memory?:

What's my favorite college memory (If I didn't go to college, then what is my favorite after high school memory?)

What's songs bring back good memories?

What did I love about my childhood?

What did I love about my teenage years?

What do I love now?:

.   .   .

If I could change anything in my life right now, what would it be?:

Is there anything I can change to make me happier?:

What are my greatest achievements?:

What give me courage?:

What gives me strength?:

What are the most important things in my life?:

What do I want others to see in me?:

What do I think about myself?:

What do I value in life?:

What is my definition of Success?:

What type of person do I want to be?:

. . .

What type of friend do I want to be?:

What Joy's do I find in Day-to-Day life?:

What do I love about work?:

What do I love about today?:

What do I love about this month?:

What do I love about this year?:

Way's I have grown over the last year:

Goals I have reached:

What I love so far about my journey:

If I could give myself advice, what would it be?:

If I gave myself a compliment, what would it be?

DAILY SELF-LOVE CHECK LIST

Meditation
Gratitude Prayer
Mental list of things I love about myself

Remember: It IS alright to have a rest
day or even a rest week. You need a
Mental recharge sometimes too.

CATEGORY	LIST THE THINGS I LOVE
I LOVE EVERYTHING ABOUT ME!	
Personality	
Eyes	
Skin	
Body	
Smile	
Teeth	
Hair	
Feet	
Mind	
I AM BEING KIND TO MYSELF	

FINAL THOUGHTS

My final thoughts on this book is this: Ultimately, life is to be enjoyed. We are meant to be playful and find happiness again. When we were younger, we didn't have to ask ourselves, "Golly, what do I want to do today that will be fun?" When we were younger, we just did it. We live our lives so free and happy when we are young. We need to find that part of youth again. When you're young, you're not even self-aware of self-love; you just naturally do it. Get back into that habit. Create a life that you want.

I wish you nothing but the best on your journey. My heart is with you, and more importantly, the Universe supports you.

Blessings,
Gabriella Starbrite
Gondora Official

ABOUT THE AUTHOR

Gabriella is a compassionate being who loves assisting others with their growth and self-awareness. To learn more about her, please visit:

www.gondoraofficial.com

There are wonderful meditations and resources on my YouTube channel

f facebook.com/gondoraofficial

⊙ instagram.com/gondoraofficial

▶ youtube.com/gondoraofficial

www.ingramcontent.com/pod-product-compliance
Lightning Source LLC
Chambersburg PA
CBHW060443040426
42331CB00044B/2515